SSICS
& CO
YCÉE

EDGAR ALLAN POE

The Fall of the House of Usher

The Tell-Tale Heart

Texte intégral
suivi d'un dossier Bac LLCER anglais

Édition annotée et commentée par
Corinne Levitt
Enseignante au Lycée ORT Villiers-le-Bel (95)

Avec une sélection d'œuvres pour constituer ton dossier et une analyse de l'axe « Imaginaires effrayants ».

Hatier

TABLE DES CRÉDITS

ILLUSTRATIONS

En 2e et 3e de couverture

- Plat 2 © Superstock/Leemage
- Plat 3 © Philippe Halsman / Magnum Photos

Dans le cahier couleur

- I © Tate, Londres, Dist. RMN-Grand Palais / Tate Photography
- II © Bridgemanimages/Leemage
- III © akg-images / Fototeca Gilardi
- IV © Birdie Thompson/AdMedia/Starface

Dans l'ouvrage

- p. 3 : © Wikipedia

TEXTES

- p. 60-61 : *Mrs Dalloway* by Virginia Woolf, 1925
- p. 61-62 : *Howl* in *Howl and Other Poems* by Allen Ginsberg © City Lights
- p. 64 : Creativity, the arts, and madness, by Maureen Neihart, September 1998 © Roeper Review, Vol. 21, No. 1, pp. 47-50. D.R.

VIDÉOS

- *House of Usher*, directed by Roger Corman, written by Richard Matheson, 1960, © ALTA VISTA PRODUCTIONS
- *Close to me*, The Cure. Music video by The Cure performing Close To Me. © 1985 Fiction Records Ltd.

Malgré nos efforts, il nous a été impossible de joindre les ayants-droit de certains documents pour solliciter l'autorisation de reproduction, mais nous avons naturellement réservé en notre comptabilité des droits usuels.

Conception et édition : Annika Sanchez, Julia Chiron
Maquette : Studio Favre & Lhaïk
Mise en page : IDT
Iconographie : Hatier Illustration

PAPIER À BASE DE FIBRES CERTIFIÉES

Hatier s'engage pour l'environnement en réduisant l'empreinte carbone de ses livres. Celle de cet exemplaire est de : 250 g éq. CO_2
Rendez-vous sur www.hatier-durable.fr

ISBN : 978-2-401-06314-3

WHO'S WHO

EDGAR ALLAN POE

Un écrivain du Sud américain

• Edgar Allan Poe naît à Boston en 1809 et meurt à Baltimore en 1849. Journaliste, poète, romancier, il est surtout connu comme auteur de contes, dans lesquels son imagination macabre préfigure certaines tendances de la littérature du XXe siècle comme la science-fiction ou encore le roman policier.

• Auteur prolifique, il ne cessera de publier poèmes et nouvelles dans les journaux de son époque. Il est considéré comme l'un des premiers écrivains américains à vivre de sa plume, même s'il passe la plus grande partie de sa vie dans la misère. Son œuvre est marquée par le sud des États-Unis dans lequel il a grandi. On y retrouve les thèmes chers à la littérature de cette région : l'obsession des crimes de famille, la puritaine scission entre le bien et du mal, la hantise de l'alcoolisme… le tout dans une ambiance fantastique et étrange. Son œuvre est souvent citée comme une influence du *Southern Gothic*.

• La France accueille très tôt l'œuvre d'Edgar Allan Poe avec enthousiasme. Les traductions que Charles Baudelaire propose au public français dès 1848 ont permis une large diffusion de l'œuvre de l'écrivain américain. Baudelaire, comme Stéphane Mallarmé et Paul Valéry après lui, voit en Poe l'archétype du poète maudit. Dans la préface du recueil *Les Histoires extraordinaires* traduit par ses soins, Baudelaire va jusqu'à dire « Les États-Unis ne furent pour Poe qu'une vaste prison qu'il parcourait avec l'agitation d'un être fait pour respirer dans un monde plus normal que cette grande barbarie éclairée au gaz ; sa vie intérieure, spirituelle de poète et même d'ivrogne n'était qu'un effort pour échapper à cette atmosphère antipathique. »

Une enfance sur les routes

• Poe naît dans une famille d'acteurs ambulants. Le père, alcoolique et tuberculeux, abandonne sa famille en 1810 et meurt quelques mois plus tard. L'alcoolisme marquera par la suite les trois enfants du couple. Elizabeth amène Edgar en Virginie, à Richmond. Il passe les premières années de sa vie dans la misère et la splendeur des décors et accessoires de théâtre. Quelques mois après leur arrivée, sa mère meurt. Poe a à peine trois ans.

• Ses deux parents décédés, Poe est recueilli par de riches négociants de Richmond, les Allan. Il devient Edgar Allan Poe – double identité décrite dans la nouvelle *William Wilson* (1839).

• En 1815, Poe quitte les États-Unis pour l'Angleterre avec ses parents adoptifs et reste quatre ans dans une pension près de Londres. Le manoir qui abrite l'école pose déjà le décor de la « Maison Usher ». Quand il rentre à Richmond, en 1820, ce fils de bonne famille joue les esthètes et les dandies. À l'université de Virginie, il joue, boit et s'endette. M. Allan se fâche et Poe fugue, fuite qu'il transposera au début de son roman *The Narrative of Arthur Gordon Pym of Nantucket* (1837).

De l'armée à la presse

• Poe a dix-huit ans et les poches vides ; il publie alors anonymement une plaquette de vers romantiques, *Tamerlane and Other Poems*. En 1827, Poe s'engage comme soldat dans l'armée fédérale sous le nom d'Edgar A. Perry. Il est cantonné en Caroline du Nord, là où il situera l'action de *The Gold-Bug* (1843). Remarqué par ses supérieurs, il entre en 1830 à l'école militaire de West Point, dont il est exclu l'année suivante. L'orphelin chassé se réfugie chez une sœur de son père biologique, Maria Clemm, dont il épousera en 1836 la fille Virginia. Le couple vit très pauvrement à Baltimore.

• Dès 1835, et jusqu'à sa mort, Poe va collaborer avec différents journaux. Il devient même directeur de la section littéraire du *Southern Literary Messenger* où son talent de polémiste et de critique est reconnu. En 1839, après avoir déménagé à Baltimore, il est nommé rédacteur du *Burton's Gentleman Magazine* dans lequel il publie certaines de ses nouvelles, dont *The Fall of the House of Usher* (1839). La revue est un vrai succès. C'est une période d'autonomie financière et de bonheur qui ne durera pas. En 1843 est publiée la nouvelle *The Tell-Tale Heart*, devenue depuis un classique de la littérature gothique.

• Il publie en 1845 son poème *The Raven*, qui assure sa renommée. Le couple Poe vit toutefois dans une grande pauvreté et déménage de ville en ville. Sa femme Virginia meurt en 1847 à l'âge de 24 ans. Il sombre encore plus dans l'alcool et tombe gravement malade. Il meurt dans des circonstances mystérieuses en 1849, à seulement 40 ans.

WHY YOU'RE GONNA LOVE THESE STORIES!

Because Edgar Allan Poe is a major American author

Vous allez découvrir l'univers gothique et effrayant d'Allan Edgar Poe, un grand auteur américain. Son influence va bien au-delà de la littérature et s'étend aux arts visuels tels que le cinéma, les séries télévisées, les dessins animés mais aussi la musique !

Because it's scary

Poe va vous entraîner au plus profond de l'âme humaine. Après avoir lu ces nouvelles, vous ne verrez plus jamais l'humanité de la même façon. Bienvenue dans un monde où se mélangent la peur, la décadence et la haine, et où la mort est souvent l'issue inévitable.

Because he invented the modern short story

Le génie littéraire de Poe consiste à mêler un style d'écriture incisif et le format de la nouvelle, un genre qui embellit ce que l'on appelle l'esthétique de la brièveté. Son style a séduit de nombreux lecteurs dans le monde entier et vous serez probablement bientôt l'un d'entre eux.

BEFORE READING

1. **Observe the front cover. What does it suggest about this book?**

2. **Study the title *The Fall of the House of Usher* closely.**
→ Explain the meaning of the name "Usher". Say what it may imply regarding the story.
→ In the title, justify the use of the word "of" between "House" and "Usher".
→ Given the elements you have just uncovered, what do you think is the meaning of the title?

3. **Study the title *The Tell-Tale Heart*.**
→ Explain and justify the wording "Tell-Tale Heart". Why do you think it was preferred to a sentence?
→ Focus on the word "tell-tale" and determine the relation between the verb and the noun.
→ Based on your understanding of the title, what can you anticipate about the content of the story?

4. **Read the back cover and say what kind of stories you are about to discover.**

THE FALL OF THE HOUSE OF USHER

Son cœur est un luth suspendu ;
Sitôt qu'on le touche il résonne.
De Béranger.

During the whole of a dull, dark, and soundless day in the autumn of the year, when the clouds hung oppressively low in the heavens, I had been passing alone, on horseback, through a singularly dreary tract of country, and at length found myself, as the shades of the evening drew on, within view of the melancholy House of Usher. I know not how it was—but, with the first glimpse of the building, a sense of insufferable gloom pervaded my spirit. I say insufferable; for the feeling was unrelieved by any of that half-pleasurable, because poetic, sentiment, with which the mind usually receives even the sternest[1] natural images of the desolate or terrible. I looked upon the scene before me—upon the mere house, and the simple landscape features of the domain—upon the bleak[2] walls—upon the vacant eye-like windows—upon a few rank sedges[3]—and upon a few white trunks of decayed trees—with an utter depression of soul which I can compare to no earthly sensation more properly than to the after-dream of the reveller[4] upon opium—the bitter lapse into every-day life—the hideous dropping off of the veil. There was

1. *les plus austères*
2. *lugubres*
3. *joncs*
4. *fêtard*

an iciness, a sinking, a sickening of the heart—an unredeemed dreariness[1] of thought which no goading of the imagination[2] could torture into aught of the sublime. What was it—I paused to think—what was it that so unnerved me in the contemplation of the House of Usher? It was a mystery all insoluble; nor could I grapple[3] with the shadowy fancies that crowded upon me as I pondered[4]. I was forced to fall back upon the unsatisfactory conclusion, that while, beyond doubt, there are combinations of very simple natural objects which have the power of thus affecting us, still the analysis of this power lies among considerations beyond our depth. It was possible, I reflected, that a mere different arrangement of the particulars of the scene, of the details of the picture, would be sufficient to modify, or perhaps to annihilate its capacity for sorrowful impression; and, acting upon this idea, I reined my horse to the precipitous brink[5] of a black and lurid tarn[6] that lay in unruffled lustre[7] by the dwelling, and gazed down—but with a shudder even more thrilling than before—upon the remodelled and inverted images of the gray sedge, and the ghastly tree-stems, and the vacant and eye-like windows.

Nevertheless, in this mansion of gloom I now proposed to myself a sojourn of some weeks. Its proprietor, Roderick Usher, had been one of my boon companions[8] in boyhood; but many years had elapsed since our last meeting. A letter, however, had lately reached me in a distant part of the country—a letter from him—which, in its wildly importunate nature, had admitted of no other than a personal reply. The MS. gave evidence of nervous agitation. The writer

1. *irrémédiable tristesse*
2. *stimulation de l'imagination*
3. *lutter contre*
4. *réfléchissais*
5. *bord escarpé*
6. *étang lugubre*
7. *éclat imperturbable*
8. *bons compagnons*

spoke of acute bodily illness—of a mental disorder which oppressed him—and of an earnest desire to see me, as his best and indeed his only personal friend, with a view of attempting, by the cheerfulness of my society, some alleviation[1] of his malady. It was the manner in which all this, and much more, was said—it was the apparent heart that went with his request—which allowed me no room for hesitation; and I accordingly obeyed forthwith[2] what I still considered a very singular summons[3].

Although, as boys, we had been even intimate associates, yet I really knew little of my friend. His reserve had been always excessive and habitual. I was aware, however, that his very ancient family had been noted, time out of mind, for a peculiar sensibility of temperament, displaying itself, through long ages, in many works of exalted art, and manifested, of late, in repeated deeds of munificent yet unobtrusive[4] charity, as well as in a passionate devotion to the intricacies[5], perhaps even more than to the orthodox and easily recognizable beauties, of musical science. I had learned, too, the very remarkable fact, that the stem[6] of the Usher race, all time-honored as it was, had put forth, at no period, any enduring branch; in other words, that the entire family lay in the direct line of descent, and had always, with very trifling[7] and very temporary variation, so lain. It was this deficiency, I considered, while running over in thought the perfect keeping of the character of the premises with the accredited character of the people, and while speculating upon the possible influence which the one, in the long lapse of centuries, might have exercised upon the other—it was this deficiency, perhaps, of

1. *soulagement*
2. *sans délai*
3. *convocation*
4. *discrète*
5. *difficultés*
6. *lignée*
7. *insignifiante*

collateral issue, and the consequent undeviating transmission, from sire to son, of the patrimony with the name, which had, at length, so identified the two as to merge the original title of the estate in the quaint[1] and equivocal appellation of the "House of Usher"—an appellation which seemed to include, in the minds of the peasantry who used it, both the family and the family mansion.

1. *bizarre*

I have said that the sole effect of my somewhat childish experiment—that of looking down within the tarn—had been to deepen the first singular impression. There can be no doubt that the consciousness of the rapid increase of my superstition—for why should I not so term it?—served mainly to accelerate the increase itself. Such, I have long known, is the paradoxical law of all sentiments having terror as a basis. And it might have been for this reason only, that, when I again uplifted my eyes to the house itself, from its image in the pool, there grew in my mind a strange fancy[2]—a fancy so ridiculous, indeed, that I but mention it to show the vivid force of the sensations which oppressed me. I had so worked upon my imagination as really to believe that about the whole mansion and domain there hung an atmosphere peculiar to themselves and their immediate vicinity[3]—an atmosphere which had no affinity with the air of heaven, but which had reeked[4] up from the decayed trees, and the gray wall, and the silent tarn—a pestilent and mystic vapor, dull, sluggish[5], faintly discernible, and leaden-hued[6].

2. *idée*
3. *alentours*
4. *empestait*
5. *apathique*
6. *couleur de plomb*

Shaking off from my spirit what must have been a dream, I scanned more narrowly the real aspect

FOCUS ON

ARRIVAL AT THE HOUSE OF USHER

P. 7 À 10 (L. 1 À 96)

Global comprehension

1 When and where is the action taking place? Justify your answer.

2 What do you know about the narrator?

3 How would you qualify the feelings expressed by the narrator in this extract?

Detailed comprehension

1 What do you think is the use of the alliteration of the sound "d" trying to produce in the first four lines of the extract? Refer to the Help Yourself.

2 Comment on the use of the colours in this passage.

3 What is the description of the house trying to suggest?

4 **[GRAMMAR]** Note the use of the past perfect continuous in the first sentence of the text (l. 3). What does it express?

> **HELP YOURSELF**
> An **alliteration** is the use of the same letter or sound, especially consonants, at the beginning of several words that are close together.
> « Live and learn » is an example of an alliteration.

Your opinion

1 What are your first impressions after reading this extract?

2 After this passage, what do you expect to uncover in the rest of the story?

3 Does the situation remind you of any other book you have read or film you have seen?

of the building. Its principal feature seemed to be that of an excessive antiquity. The discoloration of ages had been great. Minute fungi[1] overspread the whole exterior, hanging in a fine tangled web-work from the eaves. Yet all this was apart from any extraordinary dilapidation. No portion of the masonry had fallen; and there appeared to be a wild inconsistency between its still perfect adaptation of parts, and the crumbling condition[2] of the individual stones. In this there was much that reminded me of the specious totality of old wood-work which has rotted for long years in some neglected vault, with no disturbance from the breath of the external air. Beyond this indication of extensive decay, however, the fabric gave little token[3] of instability. Perhaps the cyc of a scrutinizing observer might have discovered a barely perceptible fissure, which, extending from the roof of the building in front, made its way down the wall in a zigzag direction, until it became lost in the sullen waters of the tarn.

Noticing these things, I rode over a short causeway to the house. A servant in waiting took my horse, and I entered the Gothic archway of the hall. A valet, of stealthy[4] step, thence conducted me, in silence, through many dark and intricate passages in my progress to the studio of his master. Much that I encountered on the way contributed, I know not how, to heighten the vague sentiments of which I have already spoken. While the objects around me—while the carvings[5] of the ceilings, the sombre tapestries of the walls, the ebony blackness of the floors, and the phantasmagoric armorial trophies which rattled as I strode, were but matters to which,

1. *Moisissures*

2. *état de délabrement*

3. *signe*

4. *furtif*

5. *sculptures*

or to such as which, I had been accustomed from my infancy—while I hesitated not to acknowledge how familiar was all this—I still wondered to find how unfamiliar were the fancies which ordinary images were stirring up. On one of the staircases, I met the physician of the family. His countenance, I thought, wore a mingled expression of low cunning[1] and perplexity. He accosted me with trepidation and passed on. The valet now threw open a door and ushered me into the presence of his master.

1. *ruse*

The room in which I found myself was very large and lofty. The windows were long, narrow, and pointed, and at so vast a distance from the black oaken floor as to be altogether inaccessible from within. Feeble gleams of encrimsoned[2] light made their way through the trellised panes[3], and served to render sufficiently distinct the more prominent objects around; the eye, however, struggled in vain to reach the remoter angles of the chamber, or the recesses[4] of the vaulted and fretted[5] ceiling. Dark draperies hung upon the walls. The general furniture was profuse, comfortless, antique, and tattered[6]. Many books and musical instruments lay scattered[7] about, but failed to give any vitality to the scene. I felt that I breathed an atmosphere of sorrow. An air of stern, deep, and irredeemable gloom hung over and pervaded[8] all.

2. *cramoisie*
3. *fenêtres à carreaux*
4. *renforcements*
5. *sculpté*
6. *en lambeaux*
7. *éparpillés*
8. *envahissait*

Upon my entrance, Usher rose from a sofa on which he had been lying at full length, and greeted me with a vivacious warmth which had much in it, I at first thought, of an overdone cordiality—of the constrained effort of the *ennuyé* man of the world.

A glance, however, at his countenance convinced me of his perfect sincerity. We sat down; and for some moments, while he spoke not, I gazed[1] upon him with a feeling half of pity, half of awe[2]. Surely, man had never before so terribly altered, in so brief a period, as had Roderick Usher! It was with difficulty that I could bring myself to admit the identity of the man being before me with the companion of my early boyhood. Yet the character of his face had been at all times remarkable. A cadaverousness of complexion[3]; an eye large, liquid, and luminous beyond comparison; lips somewhat thin and very pallid, but of a surpassingly beautiful curve; a nose of a delicate Hebrew model, but with a breadth of nostril unusual in similar formations; a finely moulded chin, speaking, in its want[4] of prominence, of a want of moral energy; hair of a more than web-like softness and tenuity[5];—these features, with an inordinate expansion above the regions of the temple, made up altogether a countenance not easily to be forgotten. And now in the mere exaggeration of the prevailing character of these features, and of the expression they were wont[6] to convey, lay so much of change that I doubted to whom I spoke. The now ghastly pallor of the skin, and the now miraculous lustre of the eye, above all things startled and even awed me. The silken hair, too, had been suffered to grow all unheeded[7], and as, in its wild gossamer[8] texture, it floated rather than fell about the face, I could not, even with effort, connect its Arabesque expression with any idea of simple humanity.

In the manner of my friend I was at once struck with an incoherence—an inconsistency; and I soon

1. *regardais attentivement*
2. *effroi*
3. *teint de cadavre*
4. *manque*
5. *finesse*
6. *habituées*
7. *de façon négligée*
8. *fine*

found this to arise from a series of feeble and futile struggles to overcome an habitual trepidancy—an excessive nervous agitation. For something of this nature I had indeed been prepared, no less by his letter, than by reminiscences of certain boyish traits, and by conclusions deduced from his peculiar physical conformation and temperament. His action was alternately vivacious and sullen. His voice varied rapidly from a tremulous indecision (when the animal spirits seemed utterly in abeyance[1]) to that species of energetic concision—that abrupt, weighty, unhurried, and hollow-sounding enunciation—that leaden, self-balanced and perfectly modulated guttural utterance, which may be observed in the lost drunkard, or the irreclaimable eater of opium, during the periods of his most intense excitement.

It was thus that he spoke of the object of my visit, of his earnest desire to see me, and of the solace[2] he expected me to afford him. He entered, at some length, into what he conceived to be the nature of his malady. It was, he said, a constitutional and a family evil, and one for which he despaired to find a remedy—a mere nervous affection, he immediately added, which would undoubtedly soon pass off. It displayed itself in a host of unnatural sensations. Some of these, as he detailed them, interested and bewildered me; although, perhaps, the terms and the general manner of the narration had their weight. He suffered much from a morbid acuteness of the senses; the most insipid food was alone endurable; he could wear only garments[3] of certain texture; the odors of all flowers were oppressive; his eyes were tortured by even a faint light; and there were but

1. *en suspens*

2. *réconfort*

3. *vêtements*

peculiar sounds, and these from stringed instruments, which did not inspire him with horror.

To an anomalous species of terror I found him a bounden slave. "I shall perish," said he, "I must perish in this deplorable folly. Thus, thus, and not otherwise, shall I be lost. I dread the events of the future, not in themselves, but in their results. I shudder[1] at the thought of any, even the most trivial, incident, which may operate upon this intolerable agitation of soul. I have, indeed, no abhorrence[2] of danger, except in its absolute effect—in terror. In this unnerved, in this pitiable, condition I feel that the period will sooner or later arrive when I must abandon life and reason together, in some struggle with the grim phantasm, FEAR."

I learned, moreover, at intervals, and through broken and equivocal hints[3], another singular feature of his mental condition. He was enchained by certain superstitious impressions in regard to the dwelling which he tenanted[4], and whence, for many years, he had never ventured forth—in regard to an influence whose supposititious force was conveyed in terms too shadowy here to be re-stated—an influence which some peculiarities in the mere form and substance of his family mansion had, by dint of[5] long sufferance, he said, obtained over his spirit—an effect which the physique of the gray walls and turrets[6], and of the dim tarn into which they all looked down, had, at length, brought about upon the morale of his existence.

He admitted, however, although with hesitation, that much of the peculiar gloom which thus afflicted

1. *frémis*
2. *horreur*
3. *allusions*
4. *qu'il occupait*
5. *à force de*
6. *tourelles*

him could be traced to a more natural and far more palpable origin—to the severe and long-continued illness—indeed to the evidently approaching dissolution—of a tenderly beloved sister, his sole companion for long years, his last and only relative on earth. "Her decease," he said, with a bitterness which I can never forget, "would leave him (him the hopeless and the frail) the last of the ancient race of the Ushers." While he spoke, the lady Madeline (for so was she called) passed slowly through a remote portion of the apartment, and, without having noticed my presence, disappeared. I regarded her with an utter astonishment not unmingled with[1] dread; and yet I found it impossible to account for such feelings. A sensation of stupor oppressed me as my eyes followed her retreating steps. When a door, at length, closed upon her, my glance sought instinctively and eagerly the countenance of the brother; but he had buried his face in his hands, and I could only perceive that a far more than ordinary wanness[2] had overspread the emaciated fingers through which trickled many passionate tears.

The disease of the lady Madeline had long baffled[3] the skill of her physicians. A settled apathy, a gradual wasting away of the person, and frequent although transient[4] affections of a partially cataleptical character were the unusual diagnosis. Hitherto[5] she had steadily borne up against the pressure of her malady, and had not betaken herself finally to bed; but on the closing in of the evening of my arrival at the house, she succumbed (as her brother told me at night with inexpressible agitation) to the prostrating power of the destroyer; and I learned that the glimpse I had

1. *non exempt de*

2. *pâleur*

3. *dépassé*

4. *éphémères*

5. *jusqu'à présent*

obtained of her person would thus probably be the last I should obtain—that the lady, at least while living, would be seen by me no more.

For several days ensuing, her name was unmentioned by either Usher or myself; and during this period I was busied in earnest endeavors[1] to alleviate the melancholy of my friend. We painted and read together, or I listened, as if in a dream, to the wild improvisations of his speaking guitar. And thus, as a closer and still closer intimacy admitted me more unreservedly into the recesses of his spirit, the more bitterly did I perceive the futility of all attempt at cheering a mind from which darkness, as if an inherent positive quality, poured forth upon all objects of the moral and physical universe in one unceasing radiation of gloom.

I shall ever bear about me a memory of the many solemn hours I thus spent alone with the master of the House of Usher. Yet I should fail in any attempt to convey an idea of the exact character of the studies, or of the occupations, in which he involved me, or led me the way. An excited and highly distempered ideality threw a sulphureous lustre over all. His long improvised dirges[2] will ring forever in my ears. Among other things, I hold painfully in mind a certain singular perversion and amplification of the wild air of the last waltz of Von Weber. From the paintings over which his elaborate fancy brooded[3], and which grew, touch by touch, into vagueness at which I shuddered the more thrillingly, because I shuddered knowing not why—from these paintings (vivid as their images now are before me)

1. *efforts*

2. *lamentations*

3. *ruminait*

I would in vain endeavor to educe[1] more than a small portion which should lie within the compass of merely written words. By the utter simplicity, by the nakedness of his designs, he arrested and overawed[2] attention. If ever mortal painted an idea, that mortal was Roderick Usher. For me at least, in the circumstances then surrounding me, there arose out of the pure abstractions which the hypochondriac contrived to throw upon his canvas, an intensity of intolerable awe, no shadow of which felt I ever yet in the contemplation of the certainly glowing yet too concrete reveries of Fuseli[3].

One of the phantasmagoric conceptions of my friend, partaking[4] not so rigidly of the spirit of abstraction, may be shadowed forth, although feebly, in words. A small picture presented the interior of an immensely long and rectangular vault or tunnel, with low walls, smooth, white, and without interruption or device. Certain accessory points of the design served well to convey the idea that this excavation lay at an exceeding depth below the surface of the earth. No outlet was observed in any portion of its vast extent, and no torch or other artificial source of light was discernible; yet a flood of intense rays rolled throughout, and bathed the whole in a ghastly and inappropriate splendor.

I have just spoken of that morbid condition of the auditory nerve which rendered all music intolerable to the sufferer, with the exception of certain effects of stringed instruments. It was, perhaps, the narrow limits to which he thus confined himself upon the guitar which gave birth, in great measure, to the

1. *d'en tirer*
2. *impressionnait*
3. *peintre romantique actif à la fin du XVIIIe siècle*
4. *participant*

fantastic character of the performances. But the fervid facility of his impromptus could not be so accounted for. They must have been, and were, in the notes, as well as in the words of his wild fantasias (for he not unfrequently accompanied himself with rhymed verbal improvisations), the result of that intense mental collectedness[1] and concentration to which I have previously alluded as observable only in particular moments of the highest artificial excitement. The words of one of these rhapsodies I have easily remembered. I was, perhaps, the more forcibly impressed with it as he gave it, because, in the under or mystic current of its meaning, I fancied that I perceived, and for the first time, a full consciousness on the part of Usher of the tottering[2] of his lofty reason upon her throne. The verses, which were entitled "The Haunted Palace," ran very nearly, if not accurately, thus:—

1. *recueillement*

2. *chancelante*

I.
In the greenest of our valleys,
  By good angels tenanted,
Once a fair and stately palace—
  Radiant palace—reared[3] its head.
In the monarch Thought's dominion—
  It stood there!
Never seraph[4] spread a pinion[5]
  Over fabric[6] half so fair

3. *élevait*

4. *séraphin*
5. *aile*
6. *édifice*

II.
Banners yellow, glorious, golden,
  On its roof did float and flow;

(This—all this—was in the olden
Time long ago);
And every gentle air that dallied[1],
In that sweet day,
Along the ramparts plumed[2] and pallid,
A winged odor went away.

III.
Wanderers[3] in that happy valley
Through two luminous windows saw
Spirits moving musically
To a lute's well-tunèd law;
Round about a throne, where sitting
(Porphyrogene[4]!)
In state his glory well befitting,
The ruler of the realm was seen.

IV.
And all with pearl and ruby glowing
Was the fair palace door,
Through which came flowing, flowing, flowing
And sparkling evermore,
A troop of Echoes whose sweet duty
Was but to sing,
In voices of surpassing beauty,
The wit and wisdom of their king.

V.
But evil things, in robes of sorrow,
Assailed the monarch's high estate;

1. *badinait*

2. *ornées de plumes*

3. *vagabonds*

4. *surnom attribué aux enfants d'empereur*

(Ah, let us mourn, for never morrow
Shall dawn upon him, desolate!)
And, round about his home, the glory
That blushed and bloomed
Is but a dim-remembered story
Of the old time entombed.

VI.
And travellers now within that valley,
Through the red-litten windows see
Vast forms that move fantastically
To a discordant melody;
While, like a rapid ghastly river,
Through the pale door,
A hideous throng[1] rush out forever,
And laugh—but smile no more.

I well remember that suggestions arising from this ballad, led us into a train of thought wherein there became manifest an opinion of Usher's which I mention not so much on account of its novelty (for other men have thought thus), as on account of the pertinacity[2] with which he maintained it. This opinion, in its general form, was that of the sentience[3] of all vegetable things. But, in his disordered fancy, the idea had assumed a more daring character, and trespassed, under certain conditions, upon the kingdom of inorganization. I lack words to express the full extent, or the earnest abandon of his persuasion. The belief, however, was connected (as I have previously hinted) with the gray stones of the home of his forefathers. The conditions of the

1. *foule*
2. *obstination*
3. *conscience*

sentience had been here, he imagined, fulfilled in the method of collocation of these stones—in the order of their arrangement, as well as in that of the many fungi which overspread them, and of the decayed trees which stood around—above all, in the long undisturbed endurance of this arrangement, and in its reduplication in the still waters of the tarn. Its evidence—the evidence of the sentience—was to be seen, he said, (and I here started as he spoke), in the gradual yet certain condensation of an atmosphere of their own about the waters and the walls. The result was discoverable, he added, in that silent yet importunate and terrible influence which for centuries had moulded the destinies of his family, and which made him what I now saw him—what he was. Such opinions need no comment, and I will make none.

Our books—the books which, for years, had formed no small portion of the mental existence of the invalid—were, as might be supposed, in strict keeping with this character of phantasm. We pored[1] together over such works as the "Ververt et Chartreuse" of Gresset; the "Belphegor" of Machiavelli; the "Heaven and Hell" of Swedenborg; the "Subterranean Voyage of Nicholas Klimm" by Holberg; the "Chiromancy" of Robert Flud, of Jean D'Indaginé, and of De la Chambre; the "Journey into the Blue Distance" of Tieck; and the "City of the Sun" of Campanella. One favorite volume was a small octavo edition of the "Directorium Inquisitorium," by the Dominican Eymeric de Gironne; and there were passages in Pomponius Mela, about the old African Satyrs and Œgipans, over which Usher would sit dreaming for hours. His chief delight, however, was found

1. *étudions de près*

in the perusal of an exceedingly rare and curious book in quarto Gothic—the manual of a forgotten church—the Vigiliæ Mortuorum Secundum Chorum Ecclesiæ Maguntinæ.

I could not help thinking of the wild ritual of this work, and of its probable influence upon the hypochondriac, when, one evening, having informed me abruptly that the lady Madeline was no more, he stated his intention of preserving her corpse for a fortnight[1] (previously to its final interment), in one of the numerous vaults within the main walls of the building. The worldly reason, however, assigned for this singular proceeding, was one which I did not feel at liberty to dispute. The brother had been led to his resolution (so he told me) by consideration of the unusual character of the malady of the deceased, of certain obtrusive and eager inquiries on the part of her medical men, and of the remote and exposed situation of the burial-ground of the family. I will not deny that when I called to mind the sinister countenance of the person whom I met upon the staircase, on the day of my arrival at the house, I had no desire to oppose what I regarded as at best but a harmless, and by no means an unnatural, precaution.

At the request of Usher, I personally aided him in the arrangements for the temporary entombment. The body having been encoffined, we two alone bore it to its rest. The vault in which we placed it (and which had been so long unopened that our torches, half smothered[2] in its oppressive atmosphere, gave us little opportunity for investigation) was small, damp, and entirely without means of admission for

1. *quinze jours*

2. *étouffée*

light; lying, at great depth, immediately beneath that portion of the building in which was my own sleeping apartment. It had been used, apparently, in remote feudal times, for the worst purposes of a donjon-keep, and, in later days, as a place of deposit for powder, or some other highly combustible substance, as a portion of its floor, and the whole interior of a long archway through which we reached it, were carefully sheathed with copper[1]. The door, of massive iron, had been, also, similarly protected. Its immense weight caused an unusually sharp, grating sound, as it moved upon its hinges[2].

Having deposited our mournful burden upon tressels within this region of horror, we partially turned aside the yet unscrewed lid of the coffin, and looked upon the face of the tenant. A striking similitude between the brother and sister now first arrested my attention; and Usher, divining, perhaps, my thoughts, murmured out some few words from which I learned that the deceased and himself had been twins, and that sympathies of a scarcely[3] intelligible nature had always existed between them. Our glances, however, rested not long upon the dead—for we could not regard her unawed. The disease which had thus entombed the lady in the maturity of youth, had left, as usual in all maladies of a strictly cataleptical character, the mockery of a faint blush upon the bosom and the face, and that suspiciously lingering smile upon the lip which is so terrible in death. We replaced and screwed down the lid, and, having secured the door of iron, made our way, with toil[4], into the scarcely less gloomy apartments of the upper portion of the house.

1. *recouverts de cuivre*

2. *gonds*

3. *à peine*

4. *avec difficulté*

And now, some days of bitter grief[1] having elapsed, an observable change came over the features of the mental disorder of my friend. His ordinary manner had vanished. His ordinary occupations were neglected or forgotten. He roamed[2] from chamber to chamber with hurried, unequal, and objectless step. The pallor of his countenance had assumed, if possible, a more ghastly hue—but the luminousness of his eye had utterly gone out. The once occasional huskiness[3] of his tone was heard no more; and a tremulous quaver, as if of extreme terror, habitually characterized his utterance[4]. There were times, indeed, when I thought his unceasingly agitated mind was laboring with some oppressive secret, to divulge which he struggled for the necessary courage. At times, again, I was obliged to resolve all into the mere inexplicable vagaries[5] of madness, for I beheld[6] him gazing upon vacancy for long hours, in an attitude of the profoundest attention, as if listening to some imaginary sound. It was no wonder that his condition terrified—that it infected me. I felt creeping upon me, by slow yet certain degrees, the wild influences of his own fantastic yet impressive superstitions.

It was, especially, upon retiring to bed late in the night of the seventh or eighth day after the placing of the lady Madeline within the donjon, that I experienced the full power of such feelings. Sleep came not near my couch—while the hours waned and waned away. I struggled to reason off the nervousness which had dominion over me. I endeavored to believe that much, if not all of what I felt, was due to the bewildering influence of the gloomy furniture of the room—of the dark and tattered draperies,

1. *chagrin*
2. *errait*
3. *aspect rauque*
4. *prononciation*
5. *divagations*
6. *contemplais*

which, tortured into motion by the breath of a rising tempest, swayed fitfully[1] to and fro upon the walls, and rustled uneasily about the decorations of the bed. But my efforts were fruitless. An irrepressible tremor gradually pervaded my frame; and, at length, there sat upon my very heart an incubus of utterly causeless alarm. Shaking this off with a gasp and a struggle, I uplifted myself upon the pillows, and, peering earnestly within the intense darkness of the chamber, hearkened[2]—I know not why, except that an instinctive spirit prompted me—to certain low and indefinite sounds which came, through the pauses of the storm, at long intervals, I knew not whence. Overpowered by an intense sentiment of horror, unaccountable yet unendurable, I threw on my clothes with haste (for I felt that I should sleep no more during the night), and endeavored to arouse myself from the pitiable condition into which I had fallen, by pacing rapidly to and fro[3] through the apartment.

I had taken but few turns in this manner, when a light step on an adjoining staircase arrested my attention. I presently recognized it as that of Usher. In an instant afterward he rapped, with a gentle touch, at my door, and entered, bearing a lamp. His countenance was, as usual, cadaverously wan—but, moreover, there was a species of mad hilarity in his eyes—an evidently restrained hysteria in his whole demeanor[4]. His air appalled me—but anything was preferable to the solitude which I had so long endured, and I even welcomed his presence as a relief.

1. *par intermittence*

2. *prêtais l'oreille*

3. *en faisant les cent pas*

4. *attitude*

"And you have not seen it?" he said abruptly, after having stared about him for some moments in silence—"you have not then seen it?—but, stay! you shall." Thus speaking, and having carefully shaded his lamp, he hurried to one of the casements, and threw it freely open to the storm.

The impetuous fury of the entering gust nearly lifted us from our feet. It was, indeed, a tempestuous yet sternly beautiful night, and one wildly singular in its terror and its beauty. A whirlwind[1] had apparently collected its force in our vicinity; for there were frequent and violent alterations in the direction of the wind; and the exceeding density of the clouds (which hung so low as to press upon the turrets of the house) did not prevent our perceiving the life-like velocity with which they flew careering[2] from all points against each other, without passing away into the distance. I say that even their exceeding density did not prevent our perceiving this—yet we had no glimpse of the moon or stars, nor was there any flashing forth of the lightning. But the under surfaces of the huge masses of agitated vapor, as well as all terrestrial objects immediately around us, were glowing in the unnatural light of a faintly luminous and distinctly visible gaseous exhalation which hung about and enshrouded[3] the mansion.

"You must not—you shall not behold this!" said I, shuddering, to Usher, as I led him, with a gentle violence, from the window to a seat. "These appearances, which bewilder[4] you, are merely electrical phenomena not uncommon—or it may be that they have their ghastly origin in the rank miasma

1. *tornade*

2. *se précipitant*

3. *enveloppait*

4. *déroutaient*

of the tarn. Let us close this casement;—the air is chilling and dangerous to your frame. Here is one of your favorite romances. I will read, and you shall listen:—and so we will pass away this terrible night together."

The antique volume which I had taken up was the "Mad Trist" of Sir Launcelot Canning; but I had called it a favorite of Usher's more in sad jest than in earnest; for, in truth, there is little in its uncouth[1] and unimaginative prolixity which could have had interest for the lofty and spiritual ideality of my friend. It was, however, the only book immediately at hand; and I indulged a vague hope that the excitement which now agitated the hypochondriac, might find relief (for the history of mental disorder is full of similar anomalies) even in the extremeness of the folly which I should read. Could I have judged, indeed, by the wild overstrained[2] air of vivacity with which he hearkened, or apparently hearkened, to the words of the tale, I might well have congratulated myself upon the success of my design.

I had arrived at that well-known portion of the story where Ethelred, the hero of the Trist, having sought in vain for peaceable admission into the dwelling of the hermit, proceeds to make good an entrance by force. Here, it will be remembered, the words of the narrative run thus:

"And Ethelred, who was by nature of a doughty[3] heart, and who was now mighty withal[4], on account of the powerfulness of the wine which he had drunken, waited no

1. *grossier*
2. *débordant*
3. *vaillant*
4. *en outre*

longer to hold parley with the hermit, who, in sooth[1], was of an obstinate and maliceful turn, but, feeling the rain upon his shoulders, and fearing the rising of the tempest, uplifted his mace[2] outright, and, with blows, made quickly room in the plankings of the door for his gauntleted hand; and now pulling therewith sturdily, he so cracked, and ripped, and tore all asunder, that the noise of the dry and hollow-sounding wood alarumed and reverberated throughout the forest."

At the termination of this sentence I started and, for a moment, paused; for it appeared to me (although I at once concluded that my excited fancy had deceived[3] me)—it appeared to me that, from some very remote portion of the mansion, there came, indistinctly to my ears, what might have been, in its exact similarity of character, the echo (but a stifled and dull one certainly) of the very cracking and ripping sound which Sir Launcelot had so particularly described. It was, beyond doubt, the coincidence alone which had arrested my attention; for, amid the rattling of the sashes of the casements, and the ordinary commingled noises of the still increasing storm, the sound, in itself, had nothing, surely, which should have interested or disturbed me. I continued the story:

"But the good champion Ethelred, now entering within the door, was sore enraged and amazed to perceive no signal of the

1. *en vérité*
2. *massue*
3. *trompée*

maliceful hermit; but, in the stead thereof, a dragon of a scaly and prodigious demeanor, and of a fiery tongue, which sat in guard before a palace of gold, with a floor of silver; and upon the wall there hung a shield of shining brass[1] with this legend enwritten—

Who entereth herein, a conqueror hath bin;
Who slayeth the dragon, the shield he shall win.

And Ethelred uplifted his mace, and struck upon the head of the dragon, which fell before him, and gave up his pesty breath, with a shriek so horrid and harsh, and withal so piercing, that Ethelred had fain to close his ears with his hands against the dreadful noise of it, the like whereof[2] was never before heard."

Here again I paused abruptly, and now with a feeling of wild amazement[3]—for there could be no doubt whatever that, in this instance, I did actually hear (although from what direction it proceeded I found it impossible to say) a low and apparently distant, but harsh, protracted[4], and most unusual screaming or grating sound—the exact counterpart of what my fancy had already conjured up for the dragon's unnatural shriek as described by the romancer.

Oppressed, as I certainly was, upon the occurrence of this second and most extraordinary coincidence, by a thousand conflicting sensations, in which wonder and extreme terror were predominant, I still retained

1. *cuivre*
2. *duquel*
3. *stupeur*
4. *prolongé*

sufficient presence of mind to avoid exciting, by any observation, the sensitive nervousness of my companion. I was by no means certain that he had noticed the sounds in question; although, assuredly, a strange alteration had, during the last few minutes, taken place in his demeanor. From a position fronting my own, he had gradually brought round his chair, so as to sit with his face to the door of the chamber; and thus I could but partially perceive his features[1], although I saw that his lips trembled as if he were murmuring inaudibly. His head had dropped upon his breast—yet I knew that he was not asleep, from the wide and rigid opening of the eye as I caught a glance of it in profile. The motion of his body, too, was at variance with this idea—for he rocked from side to side with a gentle yet constant and uniform sway. Having rapidly taken notice of all this, I resumed[2] the narrative of Sir Launcelot, which thus proceeded:

"And now, the champion, having escaped from the terrible fury of the dragon, bethinking himself of the brazen shield, and of the breaking up of the enchantment which was upon it, removed the carcass from out of the way before him, and approached valorously over the silver pavement of the castle to where the shield was upon the wall; which in sooth tarried not for his full coming, but fell down at his feet upon the silver floor, with a mighty great and terrible ringing sound."

1. *traits*
2. *repris*

Image 2

William Blake, ***The House of Death***
(1795-1805)

> Présentation et lecture de l'image, p. 57

Image 3

Caspar David Friedrich, ***L'Abbaye dans une forêt de chênes*** **(1809-1810)**

> Présentation et lecture de l'image, p. 57

Image 4

Antoine Wiertz, ***L'Inhumation précipitée***
(1854)

> Présentation et lecture de l'image, p. 58

Image 5

Birdie Thompson, ***Portrait de Billie Eilish*** **(2020)**

> Présentation et lecture de l'image, p. 58

No sooner had these syllables passed my lips, than—as if a shield of brass had indeed, at the moment, fallen heavily upon a floor of silver—I became aware of a distinct, hollow, metallic, and clangorous[1], yet apparently muffled, reverberation. Completely unnerved, I leaped[2] to my feet; but the measured rocking movement of Usher was undisturbed. I rushed to the chair in which he sat. His eyes were bent fixedly before him, and throughout his whole countenance there reigned a stony rigidity. But, as I placed my hand upon his shoulder, there came a strong shudder over his whole person; a sickly smile quivered about his lips; and I saw that he spoke in a low, hurried, and gibbering[3] murmur, as if unconscious of my presence. Bending closely over him, I at length drank in the hideous import of his words.

"Not hear it?—yes, I hear it, and have heard it. Long—long—long—many minutes, many hours, many days, have I heard it—yet I dared not—oh, pity me, miserable wretch that I am!—I dared not—I dared not speak! We have put her living in the tomb! Said I not that my senses were acute? I now tell you that I heard her first feeble movements in the hollow coffin. I heard them—many, many days ago—yet I dared not—I dared not speak! And now—to-night—Ethelred—ha! ha!—the breaking of the hermit's door, and the death-cry of the dragon, and the clangor of the shield!—say, rather, the rending of her coffin, and the grating of the iron hinges of her prison, and her struggles within the coppered archway of the vault! Oh! whither shall I fly? Will she not be here anon[4]? Is she not hurrying to upbraid[5] me for my haste?

1. *retentissante*

2. *bondis*

3. *bredouillant*

4. *sous peu*

5. *réprimander*

Have I not heard her footstep on the stair? Do I not distinguish that heavy and horrible beating of her heart? Madman!"—here he sprang furiously to his feet, and shrieked[1] out his syllables, as if in the effort he were giving up his soul—"Madman! I tell you that she now stands without the door!"

As if in the superhuman energy of his utterance there had been found the potency of a spell, the huge antique panels to which the speaker pointed threw slowly back, upon the instant, their ponderous[2] and ebony jaws. It was the work of the rushing gust—but then without those doors there did stand the lofty and enshrouded figure of the lady Madeline of Usher. There was blood upon her white robes, and the evidence of some bitter struggle upon every portion of her emaciated frame. For a moment she remained trembling and reeling to and fro upon the threshold[3]—then, with a low moaning cry, fell heavily inward upon the person of her brother, and in her violent and now final death-agonies, bore him to the floor a corpse, and a victim to the terrors he had anticipated.

From that chamber, and from that mansion, I fled aghast. The storm was still abroad in all its wrath as I found myself crossing the old causeway. Suddenly there shot along the path a wild light, and I turned to see whence a gleam so unusual could have issued; for the vast house and its shadows were alone behind me. The radiance was that of the full, setting, and blood-red moon which now shone vividly through that once barely-discernible fissure of which I have before spoken as extending from the roof of the

1. *hurla*

2. *lourdes*

3. *seuil*

building, in a zigzag direction, to the base. While I gazed, this fissure rapidly widened—there came a fierce breath of the whirlwind—the entire orb[1] of the satellite burst at once upon my sight—my brain reeled as I saw the mighty walls rushing asunder—there was a long tumultuous shouting sound like the voice of a thousand waters—and the deep and dank tarn at my feet closed sullenly and silently over the fragments of the "House of Usher."

1. *globe*

FOCUS ON

MADELINE'S RETURN

P. 33 À 35 (L. 796 À L. 869)

Global comprehension

1. Who is the narrator?
2. What is Rodrick's mental state at this point in the story?
3. What has actually happened to Madeline?

Detailed comprehension

1. In the first five lines of the extract (l. 796-800), notice Poe's use of the language in order to accelerate the rhythm of the story. What can you say about it?
2. Pick out a few words that highlight the macabre in the situation.
3. Explain the expression "the breaking of the hermit's door" (line 822) in the context of the story.

Your opinion

1. Did you expect the short story to end this way?
2. How is madness expressed throughout this passage? Does it scare you?

THE TELL-TALE HEART

True!—nervous—very, very dreadfully nervous I had been and am; but why will you say that I am mad? The disease had sharpened my senses—not destroyed—not dulled them. Above all was the sense of hearing acute. I heard all things in the heaven and in the earth. I heard many things in hell. How, then, am I mad? Hearken[1]! and observe how healthily—how calmly I can tell you the whole story.

1. *Prête l'oreille*

It is impossible to say how first the idea entered my brain; but once conceived, it haunted me day and night. Object there was none. Passion there was none. I loved the old man. He had never wronged me. He had never given me insult. For his gold I had no desire. I think it was his eye! yes, it was this! He had the eye of a vulture[2]—a pale blue eye, with a film over it. Whenever it fell upon me, my blood ran cold; and so by degrees—very gradually—I made up my mind to take the life of the old man, and thus rid myself of the eye forever.

2. *vautour*

Now this is the point. You fancy[3] me mad. Madmen know nothing. But you should have seen me. You should have seen how wisely I proceeded—with what caution—with what foresight—with what dissimulation I went to work! I was never kinder to the old man than during the whole week before I killed him. And every night, about midnight, I turned the latch[4] of his door and opened it—oh so gently!

3. *m'imaginez*

4. *loquet*

And then, when I had made an opening sufficient for my head, I put in a dark lantern, all closed, closed, that no light shone out, and then I thrust in my head. Oh, you would have laughed to see how cunningly I thrust it in! I moved it slowly—very, very slowly, so that I might not disturb the old man's sleep. It took me an hour to place my whole head within the opening so far that I could see him as he lay upon his bed. Ha! would a madman have been so wise as this? And then, when my head was well in the room, I undid the lantern cautiously—oh, so cautiously—cautiously (for the hinges[1] creaked)—I undid it just so much that a single thin ray fell upon the vulture eye. And this I did for seven long nights—every night just at midnight—but I found the eye always closed; and so it was impossible to do the work; for it was not the old man who vexed me, but his Evil Eye. And every morning, when the day broke, I went boldly into the chamber, and spoke courageously to him, calling him by name in a hearty tone, and inquiring how he has passed the night. So you see he would have been a very profound old man, indeed, to suspect that every night, just at twelve, I looked in upon him while he slept.

Upon the eighth night I was more than usually cautious in opening the door. A watch's minute hand moves more quickly than did mine. Never before that night had I felt the extent of my own powers—of my sagacity. I could scarcely[2] contain my feelings of triumph. To think that there I was, opening the door, little by little, and he not even to dream of my secret deeds[3] or thoughts. I fairly chuckled[4] at the idea; and perhaps he heard me; for

1. *gonds*
2. *à peine*
3. *actions*
4. *gloussai*

he moved on the bed suddenly, as if startled. Now you may think that I drew back—but no. His room was as black as pitch with the thick darkness, (for the shutters were close fastened, through fear of robbers,) and so I knew that he could not see the opening of the door, and I kept pushing it on steadily[1], steadily.

I had my head in, and was about to open the lantern, when my thumb slipped upon the tin fastening, and the old man sprang up in bed, crying out—"Who's there?"

I kept quite still and said nothing. For a whole hour I did not move a muscle, and in the meantime I did not hear him lie down. He was still sitting up in the bed listening;—just as I have done, night after night, hearkening to the death watches in the wall.

Presently I heard a slight groan, and I knew it was the groan[2] of mortal terror. It was not a groan of pain or of grief—oh, no!—it was the low stifled[3] sound that arises from the bottom of the soul when overcharged with awe. I knew the sound well. Many a night, just at midnight, when all the world slept, it has welled[4] up from my own bosom[5], deepening, with its dreadful echo, the terrors that distracted me. I say I knew it well. I knew what the old man felt, and pitied him, although I chuckled at heart. I knew that he had been lying awake ever since the first slight noise, when he had turned in the bed. His fears had been ever since growing upon him. He had been trying to fancy them causeless, but could not. He had been saying to himself—"It is nothing but the wind in the chimney—it is only a mouse crossing the floor," or "It is merely a cricket which

1. *de façon continue*
2. *grognement*
3. *étouffé*
4. *échappé*
5. *poitrine*

has made a single chirp." Yes, he had been trying to comfort himself with these suppositions: but he had found all in vain. All in vain; because Death, in approaching him had stalked with his black shadow before him, and enveloped the victim. And it was the mournful influence of the unperceived shadow that caused him to feel—although he neither saw nor heard—to feel the presence of my head within the room.

When I had waited a long time, very patiently, without hearing him lie down, I resolved to open a little—a very, very little crevice in the lantern. So I opened it—you cannot imagine how stealthily, stealthily—until, at length a simple dim ray, like the thread of the spider, shot from out the crevice[1] and fell full upon the vulture eye.

1. *fente*

It was open—wide, wide open—and I grew furious as I gazed upon it. I saw it with perfect distinctness—all a dull blue, with a hideous veil over it that chilled the very marrow in my bones; but I could see nothing else of the old man's face or person: for I had directed the ray as if by instinct, precisely upon the damned spot. And have I not told you that what you mistake for madness is but over-acuteness of the sense?—now, I say, there came to my ears a low, dull, quick sound, such as a watch makes when enveloped in cotton. I knew that sound well, too. It was the beating of the old man's heart. It increased my fury, as the beating of a drum[2] stimulates the soldier into courage.

2. *tambour*

But even yet I refrained and kept still. I scarcely breathed. I held the lantern motionless. I tried how steadily I could maintain the ray upon the eve.

Meantime the hellish tattoo[1] of the heart increased. It grew quicker and quicker, and louder and louder every instant. The old man's terror must have been extreme! It grew louder, I say, louder every moment!—do you mark me well I have told you that I am nervous: so I am. And now at the dead hour of the night, amid the dreadful silence of that old house, so strange a noise as this excited me to uncontrollable terror. Yet, for some minutes longer I refrained and stood still. But the beating grew louder, louder! I thought the heart must burst. And now a new anxiety seized me—the sound would be heard by a neighbour! The old man's hour had come! With a loud yell, I threw open the lantern and leaped into the room. He shrieked once—once only. In an instant I dragged him to the floor, and pulled the heavy bed over him. I then smiled gaily, to find the deed so far done. But, for many minutes, the heart beat on with a muffled sound. This, however, did not vex me; it would not be heard through the wall. At length it ceased. The old man was dead. I removed the bed and examined the corpse. Yes, he was stone, stone dead. I placed my hand upon the heart and held it there many minutes. There was no pulsation. He was stone dead. His eye would trouble me no more.

If still you think me mad, you will think so no longer when I describe the wise precautions I took for the concealment[2] of the body. The night waned, and I worked hastily, but in silence. First of all I dismembered the corpse. I cut off the head and the arms and the legs.

1. *battement*

2. *dissimulation*

I then took up three planks from the flooring of the chamber, and deposited all between the scantlings. I then replaced the boards so cleverly, so cunningly, that no human eye—not even his—could have detected any thing wrong. There was nothing to wash out—no stain of any kind—no blood-spot whatever. I had been too wary[1] for that. A tub[2] had caught all—ha! ha!

When I had made an end of these labors, it was four o'clock—still dark as midnight. As the bell sounded the hour, there came a knocking at the street door. I went down to open it with a light heart,—for what had I now to fear? There entered three men, who introduced themselves, with perfect suavity, as officers of the police. A shriek had been heard by a neighbour during the night; suspicion of foul play had been aroused; information had been lodged at the police office, and they (the officers) had been deputed to search the premises.

I smiled,—for what had I to fear? I bade the gentlemen welcome. The shriek, I said, was my own in a dream. The old man, I mentioned, was absent in the country. I took my visitors all over the house. I bade them search—search well. I led them, at length, to his chamber. I showed them his treasures, secure, undisturbed. In the enthusiasm of my confidence, I brought chairs into the room, and desired them here to rest from their fatigues, while I myself, in the wild audacity of my perfect triumph, placed my own seat upon the very spot beneath which reposed the corpse of the victim.

1. *méfiant*
2. *bassine*

FOCUS ON

THE HIDING OF THE BODY

P. 41 À 42 (L. 150 À L. 186)

Global comprehension

1. What is the narrator revealing in this passage?
2. What time of the day is the scene taking place? Justify the author's choice.
3. Who pays a visit to the narrator and why?

Detailed comprehension

1. Line 159, the narrator mentions an "eye" ("no human eye—not even his"). Why is the eye such an important symbol?
2. Explain the use of the simple past throughout this extract.
3. In what ways does the language (syntax, vocabulary, tenses) serve to describe the psychology of the narrator?
4. **[GRAMMAR]** Within the context of the story, explain and justify the use of the past perfect in the sentence "When I had made an end of these labors..." (p.42, l. 164).

Your opinion

1. According to you, is the narrator reliable? Why?
2. Did you enjoy the story being told from this standpoint? Why?
3. "Guilt can drive you mad". Do you agree with this expression? Discuss it from the perspective of the narrator.

The officers were satisfied. My manner had convinced them. I was singularly at ease. They sat, and while I answered cheerily, they chatted of familiar things. But, ere long, I felt myself getting pale and wished them gone. My head ached, and I fancied a ringing in my ears: but still they sat and still chatted. The ringing became more distinct:—It continued and became more distinct: I talked more freely to get rid of the feeling: but it continued and gained definiteness—until, at length, I found that the noise was not within my ears.

No doubt I now grew very pale;—but I talked more fluently, and with a heightened voice. Yet the sound increased—and what could I do? It was a low, dull, quick sound—much such a sound as a watch makes when enveloped in cotton. I gasped for breath—and yet the officers heard it not. I talked more quickly—more vehemently; but the noise steadily increased. I arose and argued about trifles[1], in a high key and with violent gesticulations; but the noise steadily increased. Why would they not be gone? I paced the floor to and fro[2] with heavy strides, as if excited to fury by the observations of the men—but the noise steadily increased. Oh God! what could I do? I foamed—I raved—I swore! I swung the chair upon which I had been sitting, and grated it upon the boards, but the noise arose over all and continually increased. It grew louder—louder—louder! And still the men chatted pleasantly, and smiled. Was it possible they heard not? Almighty God!—no, no! They heard!—they suspected!—they knew!—they were making a mockery of my horror!-this I thought, and this I think. But anything was better

1. *broutilles*

2. *faisais les cent pas*

than this agony! Anything was more tolerable than this derision! I could bear those hypocritical smiles no longer! I felt that I must scream or die! and now—again!—hark! louder! louder! louder! louder!

"Villains!" I shrieked, "dissemble no more! I admit the deed!—tear up the planks! here, here!—It is the beating of his hideous heart!"

LES DEUX NOUVELLES

p. 7 The Fall of the House of Usher
p. 37 The Tell-Tale Heart

LE DOSSIER

Pour approfondir sa lecture et se préparer pour le Bac LLCER

Analyse d'extraits / *Focus on*

p. 11 *Focus on 1 – Arrival at the house of Usher*
p. 36 *Focus on 2 – Madeline's return*
p. 43 *Focus on 3 – The hiding of the body*

Contextes

p. 48 Contexte historique et social
p. 50 Contexte artistique et littéraire

Fiches de lecture

p. 52 Fiche 1 – La nouvelle
p. 54 Fiche 2 – L'héritage littéraire et artistique d'Edgar Allan Poe

Analyse de l'image

p. 56

Axe d'étude LLCER

p. 59 Imaginaires effrayants : la folie

LE CONTEXTE
HISTORIQUE ET SOCIAL

L'expansion du territoire états-unien

• La Déclaration d'indépendance des États-Unis date de 1776 et l'indépendance est reconnue par le traité de Paris en 1783. Le pays est donc encore en pleine construction à la naissance d'Edgar Allan Poe. En 1803, Napoléon a vendu la Louisiane française à Thomas Jefferson, ce qui double la surface des États-Unis.
• En 1812, la seconde guerre d'indépendance éclate entre les troupes britanniques et canadiennes et les États-Unis. L'Empire britannique voulait empêcher les Américains de commercer avec la France et les isoler. Le conflit s'achève avec le traité de Gand, signé en 1814.
• Entre 1814 et 1858, de nombreux conflits éclatent entre les Amérindiens et le gouvernement américain. Sous la présidence d'Andrew Jackson (1829-1837), la question des *Native Americans* prend toute sa dimension. Il fait voter l'*Indian Removal Act* en 1830 pour gagner du territoire, ce qui occasionne le déplacement forcé de plusieurs peuples amérindiens. Cela causera des milliers de morts, notamment durant l'épisode du Sentier des Larmes (*Trail of Tears*).
• Enfin, en 1848, la guerre américano-mexicaine se solde par une défaite pour le Mexique, qui est amputé de la moitié de son territoire. Le Texas, annexé en 1845, et la Californie, intégrée en 1850, font dès lors partie des États-Unis.

La révolution industrielle

• Malgré les conflits, la première moitié du XIXe siècle est placée sous le signe du dynamisme économique pour les États-Unis. Les ressources naturelles foisonnent

TIMELINE

1809
Naissance d'Edgar Allan Poe

1812
Début de la seconde guerre d'indépendance

1830
Vote de l'*Indian Remova[l] Act*, déplacement forcé de milliers d'Amérindien[s]

dans le pays : gisements de charbons, minerais de fer et de cuivre. Dès 1810, les ateliers puis les usines commencent à se développer, particulièrement dans le secteur textile.

• Cette révolution industrielle s'accompagne de véritables changements concernant les modes de déplacement et de communication. Avec l'expansion territoriale, la maîtrise des voies fluviales est nécessaire. Par ailleurs, le chemin de fer s'étend progressivement sur le territoire. Les conditions sont ainsi réunies pour la maîtrise d'un espace appelé à s'étendre et pour l'expansion économique du pays.

Les mouvements sociaux et les premières vagues migratoires

• Avec le développement économique apparaissent des grèves et des émeutes, particulièrement intenses au moment de la panique bancaire qui éclate en 1837 à New York suite à une fièvre spéculative. La contestation ouvrière devient importante cette année-là, alors qu'Andrew Jackson, considéré comme populiste, termine son mandat.

• La population américaine connaît un essor démographique exceptionnel durant la première moitié du XIXe siècle : de 3, 5 millions d'habitants en 1790, la population passe à 17 millions d'habitants en 1840. À partir de 1840, l'immigration en provenance d'Europe de l'Ouest et du Nord, d'Irlande et d'Allemagne en particulier, s'intensifie.

• Les États-Unis, dans la première moitié du XIXe siècle, sont donc en proie à de grands bouleversements politiques, économiques et sociaux, qui sont associés à leur cortège d'agitation et d'instabilité, à l'image de la vie d'Edgar Allan Poe.

1837	1848	1849
Panique bancaire	**Début de la guerre américano-mexicaine**	**Mort d'Edgar Allan Poe**

Le romantisme américain

Toute la production littéraire américaine antérieure à la Guerre de Sécession (1861-1865) trouve ses racines dans le romantisme. Le romantisme américain, à l'image de son équivalent européen, est un genre artistique au sein duquel s'opposent souvent sentiments et raison. Les thématiques fondatrices du romantisme s'articulent principalement autour des axes suivants : un fond de religiosité, une affirmation individualiste, l'éloge de la nature et de l'homme simple qui y réside, le rêve, le mystère ou encore la mort.

Rip Van Winkle de Washington Irving (1819) ou *The Last of the Mohicans* de James Fenimore Cooper (1826) confirment la naissance d'une littérature romantique purement américaine. On y fait l'éloge du « bon sauvage », l'homme originel dont l'existence est en parfait accord avec la nature à l'opposé du citadin, l'homme moderne et perverti. Les transformations liées à la modernité et l'urbanisation y sont souvent dépeintes avec ironie.

La poésie américaine s'associe elle aussi rapidement au courant romantique. Le poète William Cullen Bryant va ainsi marquer les lettres américaines par son lyrisme intime et retenu. Il a puisé son inspiration dans les paysages nationaux auxquels il était tant attaché. Sa mélancolie contemplative, son goût pour la solitude et le silence des forêts ont fait de lui l'un des premiers poètes à exercer une influence dans le monde des lettres américaines. Parmi ses poèmes les plus célèbres, on peut retenir *The West Wind* (1821) ou encore *The Forest Hymn* (1824).

Le romantisme donne naissance à un sous-genre littéraire et pictural appelé le romantisme noir. Ce nouveau courant n'est autre qu'une forme exacerbée du caractère sombre du romantisme et offre une délicate fusion entre le sublime d'un côté et une fascination pour la mélancolie, et les atmosphères macabres de l'autre. On y trouve également la présence de fantômes, de vampires, de créatures surnaturelles. Dans la littérature anglo-saxonne, le romantisme noir se retrouve dans les œuvres de Mary Shelley (*Frankenstein*, 1818), de Bram Stoker (*Dracula*, 1897), et d'Edgar Allan Poe. En peinture, une des œuvres emblématique du genre est *The Nightmare* de Füssli (l'œuvre est reproduite en 2e de couverture). Poe compare d'ailleurs les inquiétants dessins de Roderick Usher à ceux du peintre dans *The Fall of the House of Usher* (p. 19, l. 360).

La peinture de paysage

Influencé par le romantisme américain, un mouvement pictural voit le jour aux États-Unis : l'*Hudson River School*. Cette école créée par Thomas Cole regroupe des peintres qui, entre les années 1820 et les années 1870, sont fascinés par les grands espaces américains et se consacrent à représenter la vallée de l'Hudson River et les montagnes du Nord-Est des États-Unis. La figuration des paysages sur des tableaux grands formats est pour eux une expression du sublime, ce concept esthétique qui considère la nature comme une manifestation de la puissance et de la bonté divine. Les paysages préservés des États-Unis étaient pour les peintres de ce mouvement comparables au paradis originel.

Le gothique américain

Au XVIIIe siècle, le roman gothique voit le jour dans une Angleterre qui se redécouvre un engouement pour l'architecture et le style médiéval. La littérature de l'époque s'interroge sur la place laissée à l'humain et ses sentiments irrationnels dans cette ère industrielle résolument pragmatique et scientifique. La littérature gothique se présente comme la forme la plus sombre du romantisme noir : autodestruction, terreur, tourments, morbidité, folie, surnaturel sont les thématiques chères aux auteurs de ce mouvement. En d'autres termes, le but du roman gothique est de faire peur. Le roman gothique anglais était très populaire au XIXe siècle aux États-Unis. Dans le contexte américain, le gothique trouve une résonance particulière en adoptant une approche psychologique, en s'intéressant aux profondeurs de l'être. Ainsi la nouvelle d'Edgar Allan Poe, *The Fall of the House of Usher*, joue sur la métaphore de la maison hantée comme représentation de l'esprit humain menacé par les peurs et les obsessions.
Le sud des États-Unis en particulier devient le terreau du gothique américain (on parle d'ailleurs de *Southern Gothic*) avec des auteurs tels que Edgar Allan Poe, puis plus tard William Faulkner ou Flannery O'Connor. L'accent est souvent mis sur les relations entre les Noirs et les Blancs et les différentes classes sociales.

FICHE 1

La nouvelle

① Un genre littéraire à part entière

La nouvelle est une œuvre littéraire en prose, proche du roman, qui s'en distingue par la brièveté, le petit nombre de personnage, la concentration et l'intensité de l'action, ainsi que le caractère insolite des événements contés. Si la nouvelle apparaît au Moyen Âge, c'est au XIXe siècle qu'elle prend son essor. En France, des auteurs tels que Honoré de Balzac, Guy de Maupassant, George Sand s'y sont adonnés.

À l'origine de la longueur d'un paragraphe, la nouvelle pouvait être publiée aussi bien dans les journaux qu'en recueil. Contrairement au roman, elle est centrée sur un seul événement et les données spatio-temporelles s'en trouvent réduites : ainsi l'action de *The Fall of the House of Usher* se déroule entre les murs d'une seule et même demeure, tandis que le récit de *The Tell-Tale Heart* se concentre sur huit nuits.

Les personnages, comme on le voit dans les deux nouvelles de Poe, sont peu nombreux : dans *The Fall of the House of Usher*, on compte seulement le narrateur – qui n'est jamais nommé –, Roderick Usher et sa sœur Madeline. La maison, lieu unique de l'action, est d'ailleurs elle-même présentée comme un personnage (« *eye-like windows* », p. 7, l. 16-17) et semble bien vivante. L'auteur détaille les lieux, mais développe peu le caractère de ses personnages. Ainsi, dans *The Tell-Tale Heart*, le narrateur et le vieil homme ne sont pas décrits.

Les nouvelles ont souvent en commun de proposer une fin inattendue, qui prend la forme d'une « chute », comme on le voit avec l'écroulement de la Maison Usher.

② Un genre prisé par les auteurs américains

Au tournant du XIXe siècle, les États-Unis sont un pays en plein essor avec des pionniers et des aventuriers qui se dirigent vers l'ouest à la recherche de nouvelles opportunités. Les journaux commandent donc aux auteurs des histoires courtes, car le constant mouvement d'une grande partie de la population américaine ne permet pas d'élaborer des histoires en feuilletons. C'est donc à cette époque que la nouvelle s'insère dans le paysage littéraire américain.

Washington Irving, puis Edgar Allan Poe et Herman Melville se sont emparés de ce genre littéraire pour créer des récits brefs, autonomes et souvent fantastiques que les lecteurs peuvent lire d'une traite. Edgar Allan Poe a d'ailleurs été le premier auteur américain à élaborer une théorie du genre, prônant une intrigue unique qui doit tout entière être tournée vers sa fin.

La nouvelle a continué à avoir sa place dans des journaux et magazines prestigieux au cours du XXe siècle, et des auteurs tels que John Steinbeck, J.D. Salinger ou Joyce Carol Oates ont été publiés dans *The Saturday Evening Post*, *The New Yorker*, *Esquire*.

③ Nouvelles policières et fantastiques

Avec *The Murders in the Rue Morgue* qu'il publie en 1841, Edgar Allan Poe fait figure de précurseur dans l'écriture de nouvelles policières. Le format bref et concis, qui force la tension et l'intrigue, se prête parfaitement aux enquêtes policières. L'auteur innove en engageant des procédés littéraires originaux tant sur le fond que sur la forme. L'écriture est incisive, presque chirurgicale et le nombre de personnages est réduit. L'esthétique de la brièveté est à son apogée. Le format court de la nouvelle est parfait pour entretenir le suspense et garder le lecteur en haleine jusqu'à la fin, qui est souvent inattendue. Les nombreuses nouvelles d'Arthur Conan Doyle, auteur de *Sherlock Holmes* (personnage créé en 1887) en sont également un bel exemple. Si la nouvelle devient une forme privilégiée de la littérature policière, elle semble aussi convenir parfaitement au genre fantastique. Les écrits d'auteurs comme H.P Lovecraft (*The Call of Cthulhu*, 1928), Isaac Asimov (*Nightfall*, 1941), ou de nos jours Stephen King (*The Man in the Black Suit*, 1994), ont fasciné et fascinent encore des générations de lecteurs. La nouvelle est un genre dont l'adaptabilité semble infinie.

FICHE 2

L'héritage littéraire et artistique d'Edgar Allan Poe

① Un auteur prolifique et un univers marquant

Edgar Allan Poe est considéré comme l'un des pères fondateurs de la littérature américaine. Auteur prolifique, il a écrit deux romans, de nombreuses nouvelles et poèmes, mais aussi des essais et des critiques littéraires. Il a créé un univers fantastique et effrayant, qui s'accorde bien avec sa personnalité mystérieuse. Son style unique et l'image d'écrivain tourmenté sont depuis rentrés dans la culture populaire américaine. L'empreinte laissée par Poe sur le monde artistique et culturel est profonde et ses héritiers sont nombreux.

② Des héritiers en littérature...

Poe a eu une très forte influence sur Charles Baudelaire, poète français et auteur du célèbre recueil *Les Fleurs du mal* (1857), qui a traduit une grande partie de son œuvre. Celle-ci a d'ailleurs été mieux reçue par le public français que le public américain et il a influencé de nombreux écrivains de par le monde, comme Stéphane Mallarmé ou Fiodor Dostoïevski, dont le roman *Crime et Châtiment* (1866) met en évidence un lien direct avec l'œuvre de Poe en abordant le côté sombre de la nature humaine. D'autres auteurs célèbres tels que H.P. Lovecraft ou Stephen King, dont les protagonistes sont souvent en proie aux méandres de leur propre santé mentale, sont également considérés comme les héritiers littéraires de Poe.

Les auteurs de romans policiers n'échappent pas non plus à son influence. Arthur Conan Doyle, en est un parfait exemple, tout comme Agatha Christie, la créatrice d'Hercule Poirot, ou encore Erle Stanley Gardner, dont le détective Perry Mason est un personnage iconique de la littérature policière américaine.

3 ... et au-delà

L'héritage artistique d'Edgar Allan Poe ne s'arrête pas au monde littéraire. En effet, le cinéma ou la musique ont très largement bénéficié de l'influence de cet écrivain devenu une référence artistique incontournable et atemporelle. *The Fall of the House of Usher* a par exemple été porté plusieurs fois à l'écran, notamment en 1960 par Roger Corman (voir p. 63). De grands noms du septième art, d'Alfred Hitchcock à Tim Burton, ont proclamé leur admiration pour Poe et se sont inspirés de son univers macabre.

Au tout début du XXe siècle, le compositeur Claude Debussy met en musique *The Fall of the House of Usher*, souhaitant en faire un opéra qu'il n'achèvera jamais. Dans les années 1980, le mouvement musical gothique reprend le flambeau : compositeurs et musiciens s'abreuvent à la source noire du maître américain. Des groupes comme Bauhaus ou The Cure (voir p. 63) développent un univers sombre et mélancolique, proche des névroses littéraires développées chez Edgar Allan Poe. Sur une tonalité plus *hard rock*, le groupe Iron Maiden a intitulé une de ses chansons *Murders in the Rue Morgue*. Plus récemment, c'est la jeune auteure-interprète californienne Billie Eilish qui reprend le flambeau en composant un album inspiré de terreurs nocturnes et de rêves lucides où se mêlent des thèmes chers à Edgar Allan Poe : le chagrin, la solitude, le suicide, la toxicomanie ou encore la santé mentale.

Au-delà du cinéma et de la musique, c'est toute la culture populaire américaine qui se voit influencée par l'œuvre de Poe. Aucun domaine n'est en reste : l'illustration, avec l'univers gothique de *The Addams Family* créée par Chas Addams et qui sera adaptée en série et en films, ou plus récemment la série *American Horror Story*. Les dessins animés et même les jeux vidéo reprennent des thèmes, des idées et des personnages inspirés de l'univers de l'écrivain. C'est le cas des *Simpsons* avec l'épisode spécialement conçu pour Halloween *Treehouse of Horror*, dont l'un des segments est une adaptation de *The Raven*, célèbre nouvelle de Poe, ou *The Dark Eye* un jeu largement inspiré de plusieurs de ses nouvelles dont *The Tell-Tale Heart*.

Certains thèmes caractérisent l'œuvre d'Edgar Allan Poe : l'abandon, l'isolement, les phobies, l'addiction ou encore la confrontation avec la mort. La fragilité psychologique de l'auteur, due à une existence troublée, explique en partie la prévalence de ces thématiques dans son œuvre. Poe n'est toutefois pas le seul auteur à être hanté par ces peurs morbides. D'autres artistes ont comme lui fait le choix de figurer par l'art, notamment visuel, les faces obscures de l'âme humaine.

1 ***The Nightmare*** (1781)

→ Auteur : Johann Heinrich Füssli (1741-1825), peintre anglais d'origine suisse
→ Technique : peinture
→ Dimensions : 101, 6 x 127 cm

L'œuvre est reproduite en 2e de couverture

Ce tableau représente une femme endormie sur un lit, la tête penchée vers le bas. Sur sa poitrine se tient un démon qui nous regarde. À l'arrière-plan, on peut voir la tête d'un cheval aux yeux argentés qui émerge d'un rideau de velours rouge. La toile semble dépeindre une femme en train de rêver, et le contenu même de son cauchemar.

LIRE L'IMAGE

1. Que suggère la position de la femme ?
2. Quels sont les éléments du tableau qui appartiennent au monde réel et quels sont ceux qui appartiennent au monde du rêve ?
3. Edgar Allan Poe cite le peintre Füssli dans la nouvelle *The Fall of the House of Usher* (p. 19, l. 360). Selon vous, pourquoi ?

② *The House of Death* (1795-1805)

→ Auteur : William Blake (1757-1827), peintre et poète anglais
→ Technique : aquarelle et encre
→ Dimensions : 48,5 x 61 cm

L'œuvre est reproduite dans le cahier couleur, p. I

Cette œuvre est une illustration du poème *Paradise Lost* de John Milton, que William Blake considérait comme le plus grand poète anglais. On y voit l'archange Michel qui montre à Adam la misère qui sera infligée à l'homme après avoir mangé le fruit défendu.

LIRE L'IMAGE

1. Qu'évoque pour vous cette image ?
2. Quels éléments visuels symbolisent la mort ?
3. De quelle manière le religieux s'exprime-t-il à travers cette œuvre ?

③ *L'Abbaye dans une forêt de chênes* (1809-1810)

→ Auteur : Caspar David Friedrich (1774-1840), peintre et dessinateur allemand
→ Technique : peinture
→ Dimensions : 110 x 171 cm

L'œuvre est reproduite dans le cahier couleur, p. II

Une procession de moines se dirige vers le portail d'une église en ruine de style gothique. Certains portent un cercueil. La partie inférieure de la scène est plongée dans l'obscurité.

LIRE L'IMAGE

1. Observez la peinture. Quels en sont les enjeux principaux ?
2. Selon vous, que s'apprêtent à faire les moines ?
3. À votre avis, quels sentiments souhaite exprimer Caspar David Friedrich ?

④ *L'Inhumation précipitée* (1854)

→ **Auteur** : Antoine Wiertz (1806-1865), peintre et sculpteur belge
→ **Technique** : peinture
→ **Dimensions** : 160 x 235 cm

L'œuvre est reproduite dans le cahier couleur, p. III

Sur cette peinture on voit un homme, l'œil exorbité et la bouche béante, qui tente d'ouvrir le cercueil dans lequel il se trouve. On peut y lire une inscription : *Mort du choléra, certifié par nous, docteurs.* Ce tableau exprime la hantise de se faire enterrer vivant.

LIRE L'IMAGE

❶ Selon vous, pour quelle raison l'homme a-t-il été enterré vivant ?
❷ Quelle atmosphère se dégage de ce tableau ?
❸ Quels sont les points communs entre cette peinture et les deux nouvelles d'Edgar Allan Poe que vous avez lues ?

⑤ *Portrait de Billie Eilish* (2020)

→ **Auteure** : Birdie Thompson, photographe américaine
→ **Technique** : photographie

L'œuvre est reproduite dans le cahier couleur, p. IV

Billie Eilish est une jeune auteure-compositrice-interprète américaine célèbre pour sa chanson *Bad Guy*. Elle a développé un univers étrange et s'exprime souvent au sujet de la dépression et des troubles mentaux.

LIRE L'IMAGE

❶ Observez en détail la tenue vestimentaire de la chanteuse. Comment la qualifieriez-vous ? Quel lien y voyez-vous avec le mouvement gothique ?
❷ Que suggère son regard et plus généralement l'expression de son visage ?

Imaginaires effrayants : la folie

L'étude de The Fall of the House of Usher *et* The Tell-Tale Heart *s'inscrit dans la thématique* Imaginaires *du programme de première LLCER. Plus précisément, ces œuvres illustrent l'axe d'étude « Imaginaires effrayants ».*

Les deux œuvres de Poe mettent chacune en scène la folie d'un personnage. De l'Antiquité à nos jours, la folie a toujours trouvé sa place dans le monde des arts et de la littérature. Qu'il s'agisse de troubles obsessionnels, de phobies, de pathologies affectant les facultés mentales, de l'exaltation des émotions ou des sens, la folie maladive ou passagère est un thème artistique récurrent. La face sombre de l'âme humaine est souvent dépeinte par les artistes et est une source d'inspiration inépuisable. La notion de folie induit un questionnement multiple autour de l'œuvre et sa création. Est-ce l'auteur qui est fou ou bien ses personnages ? Existe-il une interaction entre les deux ?

La folie revêt des formes innombrables et peut entraîner des événements tragiques. C'est pourquoi les différents arts, en donnant une forme esthétique à une réalité triste et parfois dramatique, apportent consolation et espoir. Des artistes, comme Edgar Allan Poe, Virginia Woolf ou Salvador Dalí, en s'inspirant de cette thématique atemporelle, n'ont-ils pas ainsi trouvé le moyen d'exorciser leurs propres démons ?

❶ VIRGINIA WOOLF, **MRS DALLOWAY**, 1925

Ce roman nous fait pénétrer dans l'intimité de l'univers psychologique d'une femme de la haute société londonienne au lendemain de la première guerre mondiale. À travers ce roman, Woolf aborde plusieurs facettes de la maladie mentale comme la bipolarité, le choc post-traumatique ou encore le suicide.

Septimus Warren Smith, aged about thirty, pale-faced, beak-nosed, wearing brown shoes and a shabby overcoat, with hazel eyes which had that look of apprehension in them which makes complete strangers apprehensive too. The world has raised its whip; where will it descend?

Everything had come to a standstill. The throb of the motor engines sounded like a pulse irregularly drumming through an entire body. The sun became extraordinarily hot because the motor car had stopped outside Mulberry's shop window; old ladies on the tops of omnibuses spread their black parasols; here a green, here a red parasol opened with a little pop. Mrs. Dalloway, coming to the window with her arms full of sweet peas, looked out with her little pink face pursed in enquiry. Every one looked at the motor car. Septimus looked. Boys on bicycles sprang off. Traffic accumulated. And there the motor car stood, with drawn blinds, and upon them a curious pattern like a tree, Septimus thought, and this gradual drawing together of everything to one centre before his eyes, as if some horror had come almost to the surface and was about to burst into flames, terrified him. The world wavered and quivered and threatened to burst into flames. It is I who am blocking the way, he thought. Was he not being looked at and pointed at; was he not weighted there, rooted to the pavement, for a purpose? But for what purpose?

"Let us go on, Septimus," said his wife, a little woman, with large eyes in a sallow pointed face; an Italian girl.

But Lucrezia herself could not help looking at the motor car and the tree pattern on the blinds. Was it the Queen in there—the Queen going shopping?

The chauffeur, who had been opening something, turning something, shutting something, got on to the box.

"Come on", said Lucrezia.

But her husband, for they had been married four, five years now, jumped, started, and said, "All right!" angrily, as if she had interrupted him.

People must notice; people must see. People, she thought, looking at the crowd staring at the motor car; the English people, with their children and their horses and their clothes, which she admired in a way; but they were "people" now, because Septimus had said, "I will kill myself"; an awful thing to say. »

2 ALLEN GINSBERG, **HOWL**, 1956

Ce long poème très controversé est l'un des plus célèbres de la littérature américaine. Son auteur, Allen Ginsberg, a été une grande figure de la *Beat Generation* dans les années 1950-1960. *Howl* traite principalement de la folie dans une société dominée par le besoin de se conformer aux normes. Cet extrait correspond aux premières lignes du poème.

« I saw the best minds of my generation destroyed by madness, starving hysterical naked,
dragging themselves through the negro streets at dawn looking for an angry fix,
angelheaded hipsters burning for the ancient heavenly connection to the starry dynamo in the machinery of night,

who poverty and tatters and hollow-eyed and high sat up smoking in the supernatural darkness of cold-water flats floating across the tops of cities contemplating jazz,

who bared their brains to Heaven under the El and saw Mohammedan angels staggering on tenement roofs illuminated,

who passed through universities with radiant cool eyes hallucinating Arkansas and Blake-light tragedy among the scholars of war,

who were expelled from the academies for crazy & publishing obscene odes on the windows of the skull,

who cowered in unshaven rooms in underwear, burning their money in wastebaskets and listening to the Terror through the wall,

who got busted in their pubic beards returning through Laredo with a belt of marijuana for New York,

who ate fire in paint hotels or drank turpentine in Paradise Alley, death, or purgatoried their torsos night after night ”

3 PHILIPPE HALSMAN, **PORTRAIT DE SALVADOR DALÍ**, 1954

Philippe Halsman est un photographe qui a travaillé pour de grands magazines américains tels que *Time* ou *Life*. Il a également collaboré pendant plus de 30 ans avec Salvador Dalí, le célèbre peintre et sculpteur espagnol, avec qui il a expérimenté des mises en scène photographiques audacieuses.

L'œuvre est reproduite en 3e de couverture

❹ ROGER CORMAN, **HOUSE OF USHER**, 1960

Vidéo
Extrait de film - 1:26
hatier-clic.fr/ccfal01

En 1960, le réalisateur américain Roger Corman porte à l'écran un film inspiré de la nouvelle d'Edgar Allan Poe.

❺ THE CURE, **CLOSE TO ME**, 1985

Vidéo
Extrait de clip - 3:46
hatier-clic.fr/ccfal02

Le groupe de rock anglais The Cure est célèbre dans le monde entier pour sa chanson *Close to me*. Le clip qui a accompagné sa sortie nous présente un univers claustrophobe, morbide, proche de la folie. Les interprètes se retrouvent enfermés dans une armoire qui tombe d'une falaise dans la mer.

❻ MAUREEN NEIHART, **CREATIVITY, THE ARTS, AND MADNESS**, 1998

Dans cet article publié dans une revue médicale, la psychologue américaine Maureen Neihart tente de comprendre le lien entre la créativité artistique et la folie.

This article explores studies on the link between creativity and madness. It explains that there definitely is a more frequent occurrence of certain types of mental problems in those who are exceptionally creative. It also brings up questions such as whether the creativity causes the higher incidence of mental illness or vice versa. [...]
"Men have called me mad; but the question is not yet settled, whether madness is or is not the loftiest intelligence–whether much that is glorious–whether all that is profound–does not spring from disease of thought-from moods of mind exalted at the expense of the general intellect. They who dream by day are cognizant of many things which escape those who dream only by night. In their grey vision they obtain glimpses of eternity.... They penetrate, however rudderless or compassless, into the vast ocean of the light affable." (Edgar Allan Poe)
The belief that madness is linked with creative thinking has been held since ancient times. It is a widely popular notion. Deviant behavior, whether in the form of eccentricity or worse, is not only associated with persons of genius or high-level creativity, but it is frequently expected of them. Since the time of the Greek philosophers, those who wrote about the creative process emphasized that creativity involves a regression to more primitive mental processes, that to be creative requires a willingness to cross and recross the lines between rational and irrational thought. What is the evidence that there is a link between creativity and madness? What account can be given for this link, biologically and psychologically? And what does this association suggest for related research and our understanding of creative people? The aim of this article is to describe what creativity and madness have in common and to discuss implications for creative thinking in gifted education. The article begins with a brief, historical overview of the topic, followed by some highlights of studies on creativity and mental illness. Explanations for the possible link between creativity and madness are then addressed. Creativity is defined as the production of something that is both new and valued and madness is defined as a self-destructive deviation in behavior. The article concludes with a discussion of implications for the creative process in gifted education and questions for further research.

Achevé d'imprimer en France par Dupliprint - 733, rue Saint-Léonard - 53100 Mayenne
N° d'impression : 2989704N - Dépôt légal n° 06314-3/04 - mai 2024
IMPRIM'VERT®